HOW TO MAKE YOUR
OWN MONSTER MOVIES

Stephen Mooser

Julian Messner New York

Library of Congress Cataloging in Publication Data

Mooser, Stephen.
   Lights! camera! scream!

   Includes index.
   Summary: Reveals the secrets behind creating monsters
and bringing them to life on the screen.
   1. Horror films — Production and direction — Juvenile
literature.   [1. Horror films — Production and direction.
2. Motion pictures — Production and direction]
I. Ezmirlian, John, ill.   II. Title.
PN1995.9.H6M56   1983   792'.023   83-13324
ISBN 0-671-43017-3

Acknowledgments

Special thanks to Nora Serra and her students
at Oneonta School in Pasadena, California

For
Greg Mooser
Jonathan Mooser

Also by Stephen Mooser
Monster Fun

CONTENTS

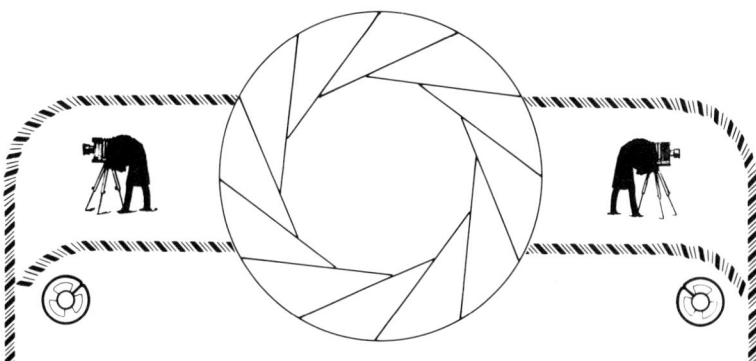

INTRODUCTION

Making Your Own Monster Movies

King Kong, Godzilla, the Alien—when we think of monsters, we often think first of the creatures we've seen in the movies. We remember these frightening characters because they seemed so real the first time we saw them on the screen. Like modern-day Dr. Frankensteins, filmmakers are constantly unleashing monsters into the world.

Of course, filmmakers don't really create living, breathing monsters. They only make it seem that way. Through the use of camera tricks, miniature sets, and special effects, they can do such wonders as turn an ordinary garden lizard into a twenty-foot dinosaur, send a rocketship to the stars, make skeletons dance, and shrink a man to the size of an ant. What seems like magic to the moviegoer is mostly the result of hard work and patience on the part of the people who make the movies. Their special effects wizardry is the subject of this book.

We are going to take a look at how movie monsters are made and, at the same time, show you how to make monster movies of your own. It is not as difficult as you might think. In fact, the first films we will make don't even require a camera. This book will reveal the secrets behind the monster-maker's magic. You will see how to create the monsters, and then how to bring them to life on the screen in all their terrible glory.

MAKING MOVIE MAGIC

How Special Effects Experts
Create Monsters For The Movies

Movies can yank you back into time, propel you far into the future, take you anywhere and show you anything the mind can imagine. These unique qualities make them the perfect breeding ground for monsters. Where else but on film can you see such wonders as a fleet of Martian spaceships destroying Los Angeles, a ten-story-tall lizard stomping his way through Tokyo, or a herd of one-ton ants eating their way through a desert town? Monsters and movies just seem to go together and, since the dawn of the cinema, filmmakers have been filling theaters with all kinds of horrible, hideous creatures.

Of course, filmmakers haven't just gone out to find creepy creatures to cast in their films. They have had to find ways to show their fantasies on the screen without letting the audience know that everything was faked.

Over the years special effects experts have developed a number of techniques that enable filmmakers to show almost anything a film writer could dream up. Some of these techniques may be too difficult for you to use when you make your own movie, but others may be just right for the type of film you want to do.

The earliest special effect trick was called the *matte*. Basically it is the same as cutting up two photos and combining them onto one sheet. Say

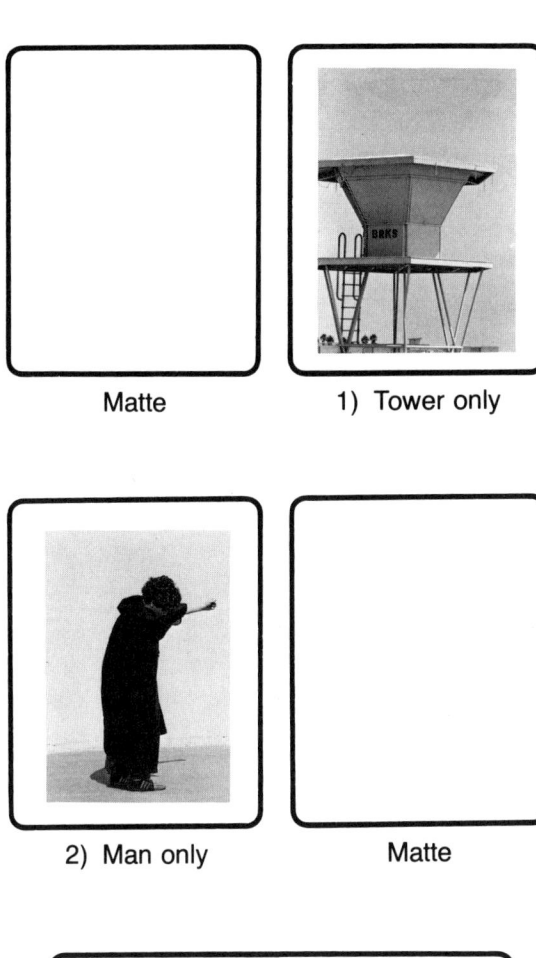

Matte   1) Tower only

2) Man only   Matte

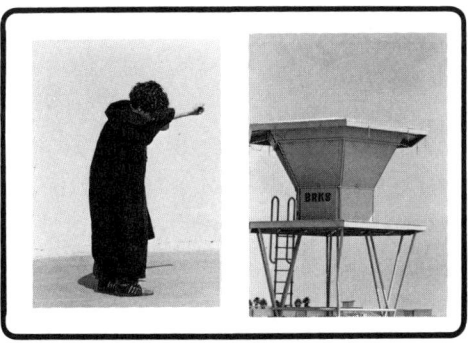

3) Finished shot

you wanted to show a twenty-foot man standing next to a tower. You would start off by covering half your camera lens with a piece of black paper called a matte. Then you would shoot a picture of the tower, exposing only half the film. You would then wind the film back and cover the other side of the lens. Then you would shoot a picture of a man standing in an open field. When the film is developed, the tower and the man will appear side by side and the man will look like a giant, standing as tall as the tower.

Another early special effects trick, and one still in use today, is the painted glass matte. For this effect an artist would paint part of a scene on a piece of clear glass. Then the camera would shoot through the glass and the painting would be included in the scene. Universal Studios' most recent remake of *Dracula* featured a magnificent castle. But that castle exists only on a glass matte painted by Albert Whitlock, the recognized master of the glass matte. To create Dracula's castle, Whitlock painted a precisely detailed picture of the famous bloodsucker's residence on a piece of glass. Then, with the glass portrait properly positioned in front of the lens, the camera was pointed at a nearby hill. When the film was developed, the hill and the castle were one and Dracula had a home. This is how it was done:

14

1) Glass matte

2) Shooting through matte picture of castle toward a distant hill.

3) Finished picture

In Alfred Hitchcock's horror classic, *The Birds*, the director made effective use of two of the most popular monster-movie effects. One was rear projection and the other was a mechanical miniature.

In *rear projection*, part of the scene is projected from behind the actors onto a screen. Since the projector is behind the action, the actors' shadows don't show up on the screen. *The Birds* was full of scenes of people running from attacks of thousands of crazed birds. Most of these scenes were done with rear projection. A flock of birds was filmed in an open field. Then, in a studio, actors were shown running in front of the screen showing the birds. To the untrained eye it appeared as if the birds and the people were in the same place.

Hitchcock also made use of *mechanical miniature*—birds in this film. Many of the birds shown pecking people's heads or banging on their windows were just small feathered toys. Those birds were a director's dream. They always performed on cue, and they worked for free.

Miniature sets and detailed models are probably the most common effects found in today's monster and science fiction movies. Though Godzilla appears to be several stories tall, in most scenes he's just a man in a costume walking around in a miniature set. When the giant lizard smashes a house and steps on a car, he's really only knocking over a dollhouse and squashing a toy automobile. On the other hand, for films like *Gulliver's Travels* and *The Incredible Shrinking Man*, the studios built giant chairs and tables, even huge dishes and glasses, in order to make normal-sized people appear incredibly tiny.

In 1914, a young man named Willis O'Brien produced a one-minute movie called *The Dinosaur and The Missing Link*. It was the first real monster movie to use the technique of *stop-frame model animation*. O'Brien got his animation ideas from the cartoon makers. But, instead of animating his picture with drawings, he animated it with a clay model—in this instance a dinosaur.

Cartoons are really nothing more than a series of individual pictures, each one a little different from the one before it. When the pictures are projected rapidly, one after another, it appears as if the subject is moving. A strip of cartoon might look something like the illustration on the next page.

For his technique of stop-frame animation, O'-Brien put his small clay dinosaur in front of a realistic picture of a jungle and then began to film it. He would snap off one or two frames of film, move his dinosaur's head and legs just slightly, take another

Notice how the flying saucer moves
across the frame. When the cartoon is
shown, the saucer will look as
if it is zipping across the sky.

two shots, and so on. It took him hours just to get his model from one end of the jungle to the other, but when the film was shown it looked as if his dinosaur was actually walking.

O'Brien went on to make scores of films using this technique, including the great *King Kong*, in which he was called on to animate a model of the giant ape in a number of scenes.

O'Brien's star pupil, Ray Harryhausen, is today's master of the stop-action model technique. He has animated hundreds of Hollywood's most famous monsters such as the warty cyclops in the *Seventh Voyage of Sinbad*, the lizardlike Ymir in *Twenty Million Miles To Earth*, the giant crabs in *Mysterious Island*, the skeleton soldiers in *Jason and the Argonauts*, and the winged Pegasus in *Clash of The Titans*.

Someone once said that pictures don't lie, but a special effects expert will tell you differently. In the following pages you'll learn some of the tricks that will enable you to create the monster of your dreams, and then to make him real enough to haunt the nightmares of others. There is nothing to stop you but your imagination. And this book will tell you all you need to know to put that imagination on film.

What kind of monster movie would you like to make? Will it be an outer space epic on a faraway planet, or a prehistoric jungle picture that takes place in earth's distant past? Will you use picture animation, model animation, or a combination of these and others? Will you need to make sets? Put together costumes? Find a willing lizard? Remember, with special effects anything is possible. Let your imagination go. Before you know it, you'll be the one sitting behind the camera and yelling, "Lights! Camera! Scream!"

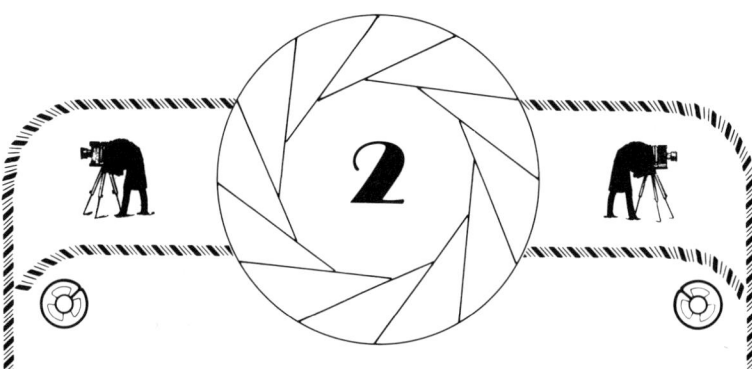

FLIP PICTURES

Making Monster Movies
Without A Camera

Monster movies come in all shapes and sizes. There are the Hollywood extravaganzas that cost millions of dollars and take years to make. And then there are others, such as flip pictures, that cost less than a dollar and can be made in under an hour. Since you probably don't have either a year or a million dollars to spend on your movie, let's begin with the flip-picture monster movie.

Flip pictures are so simple that you won't even need a camera to make them or a projector to show them. They have been around for hundreds of years. They are really quite easy to make. All you need is:

- A PACK OF 25–50 STIFF THREE-BY-FIVE-INCH CARDS (Unlined index cards are good)

- A BALL-POINT OR FELT-TIP PEN (Any dark color is fine)

Hold the cards in your hand and flip through them with your thumb as you would a deck of cards. Notice that you will be able to see about one-third of the surface of the card clearly. This will be the part of the card you will use to make your flip movie. The middle surface of the card will always be blank. Flip movies go by so fast and are so short that it is important to keep the drawing and the action as simple as possible.

As a start let's make a flip movie showing a rocket ship blasting off for the moon.

Begin by drawing a rocket ship pointing up at the moon on the top card. It should look something like this:

To make the pictures seem to move smoothly it is best to repeat each picture once. So, on the next card in the deck, draw an identical picture of the moon and the rocket ship.

As you work your way through the deck of cards, slowly advance your rocket ship, about a quarter of an inch, every two pictures. As an extra touch add some smoke and fire coming out of the ship's exhaust as it lifts off its launching pad.

Finally, have your ship either land or crash on the moon. The whole journey should take about 25 cards to complete. When the drawings are done, assemble them in the proper order and flip them with your thumb. Your rocket ship will perform just as you drew it.

Congratulations! You've just made your first movie.

By turning your deck of cards over, and around, you will have space for three more flip movies. Remember to keep the action simple. Make your own stories or use one of these:

Birth Of The Wolf Creature

A happy, smiling face is slowly covered with wild hair and the teeth grow into long, sharp fangs.

Attack Of The Bug-Eyed Thing From Outer Space

A tiny dot grows and grows till it fills up half the card. As it gets larger we see that it is a warty, bug-eyed creature.

Earthquake!

Two tall buildings shake back and forth till they collapse in a cloud of dust and rubble.

DRAWING ON FILM

More Monster Movies Without A Camera

Simple monster movies can be made by drawing directly onto the film. You'll need a projector to show the final product, but you won't need a camera to film it.

What you will need in addition to the projector is:

- A FIFTY-FOOT ROLL OF SUPER-8 CLEAR LEADER. The leader is the lead or beginning part of the film, the part, usually transparent, that is first threaded into the projector. If you can't get a roll of clear leader at a large camera store, you may have to buy a roll of film and have it developed as it is—before you take any pictures. If you haven't exposed it, the roll will come back clear.

- BLACK PELIKAN-T INDIA INK. Available at art supply stores. The "T" means that the ink is made especially for drawing on plastic.

- INK PEN WITH FINE POINT. Also from art supply stores.

- A MAGNIFYING GLASS ON A STAND. This will help you to see your work as you draw as everything is very small. The magnifying glass is not essential, but is helpful.

After you have assembled your materials you will need a place to work. A desk or drawing table that is well lighted is best. Tape down a sheet of white construction paper on top of the desk. Next, unwind some of the film from the reel and tape it down to the construction paper with clear tape.

Super-8 film is shown on the screen at 18 frames per second. In other words, someone watching a movie sees 18 individual frames (or pictures) each second. Eighteen frames may take a long time to draw, but will only take one second to run through the projector. So your first film may only last four or five seconds. Nevertheless, a film of this length will require from 70 to 100 individual drawings. This won't be as hard as it sounds if you keep your story and drawings simple.

The film is taped firmly to the table as the boy draws on film.

Before you begin to draw on your film you need to do a little planning. Think up a very simple story and write it down on a piece of paper. You are going to be drawing on a very small area so keep your drawings simple, too. Let's say you choose to show a magic wand making someone disappear. It's a simple story, and the drawings, a wand and a head, will be simple, too.

Next you need to make a *storyboard*, or cartoon strip, of your story to work from. Your storyboard is your script, in cartoon form. Here is a rough storyboard of the above story. Note how all the important action is drawn in. As with the flip pictures be sure that each frame advances the story slightly. In sequence number two, following the titles, we see the wand slowly coming into the scene. In sequence number three it slowly descends toward the head and in number seven and eight the head is dissolving.

Now draw what is on the storyboard onto the film. The number of frames for each sequence is just a suggestion. It is approximately the number of pictures you will need to draw to get from one part of the action to the next. Experiment, if you wish. You might want to speed up the action by drawing fewer frames or slow it down by adding more drawings.

1) Title—12 frames

2) Wand appears—
12 frames

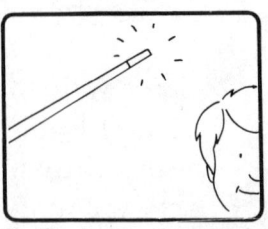

3) Boy's head comes into
frame—12 frames

4) Boy's head closer to
wand—12 frames

5) Wand touches boy—
12 frames

6) Wand withdrawn
slowly—12 frames

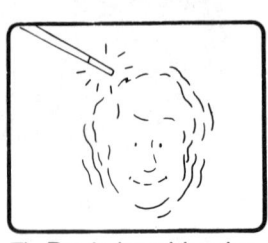

7) Boy's head begins to
get fuzzy—12 frames

8) Boy's head gone in a
cloud—12 frames

9) End title—12 frames

Now all you have to do is thread your film into your projector and the show is on.

Camera stores also sell rolls of all-white leader. You can make a film with this kind of leader, too. Again, tape down the leader to the table. But this time, instead of drawing on film, you scratch out the white paint with a pin or the end of a paperclip. If you wish, you can color in the lines you have scratched out with colored Pelikan-T ink. When projected, the figures you scratched out will seem to move against a black background.

Think up some simple monster movies you'd like to make by drawing on film. You may want to use some of the ideas suggested for the flip movies, or you might want to make one of these creepy flicks:

Attack Of The Giant Worm

Some cars are going down a road. Suddenly a giant worm comes up out of the ground and swallows up the cars—and the highway, too.

Advance your car and worm slightly every two frames.

Creature From The Deep

A boat is floating on a little pond or out at sea. Suddenly the water begins to bubble and foam. A long-necked creature rises up out of the deep. The person in the boat sees the creature and quickly rows away.

Advance your boat and creature slightly every two frames.

Take your time. Professional movie makers work long and hard on their films. You should, too. The more time you take to plan and draw your film the better it will look when it is done. Clean up when you are done. Put away all your inks and wash your pens and brushes. After your drawings have dried (fifteen–thirty minutes), roll the film onto the reel so that it doesn't get dusty or scratched.

4

BASIC
MOVIE-MAKING
EQUIPMENT

A Few Things You'll Need To
Turn Your Nightmares Into
Reality

If you want to go beyond flip pictures and draw-ings on film, you are going to need to buy or borrow some basic filmmaking equipment. The most im-portant things you'll need are:

- A CAMERA. The most inexpensive and practical camera for the type of work you will be doing is the Super-8. It is the most common movie cam-era in use today. If your family doesn't already own a Super-8 camera, see if you can borrow one from a friend or from your school.

If you have to buy a new or used Super-8 camera, make sure that the one you buy has the following features:

CABLE RELEASE. Most cameras can be bought with a cable that extends from the camera. When you push the button at the end of this cable, one frame of film is exposed. This allows you to snap off one or two pictures without touching, and possibly shaking, the camera itself. Animation work re-quires that the camera remain stationary for long periods of time. If the camera moves during film-ing, you'll get a jerky picture.

CLOSE-UP LENS. If your camera isn't already fit-ted with a close-up lens, it would be a good idea to purchase an inexpensive one. Animation requires lots of close-up work, and you want your miniature sets and characters to be in focus.

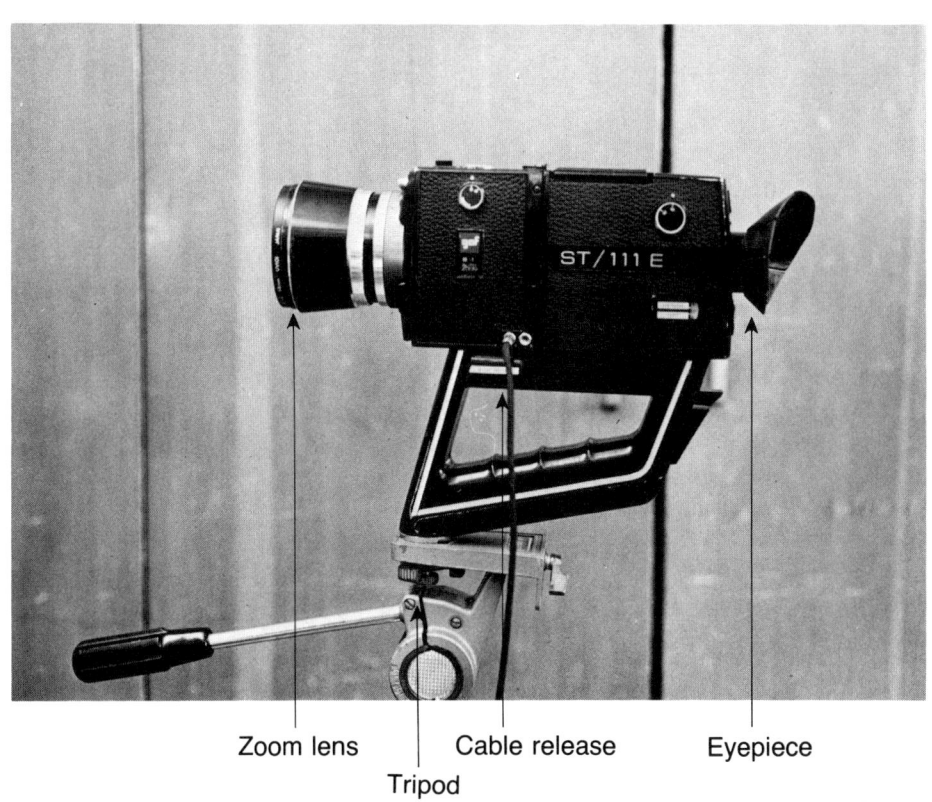

Zoom lens | Cable release   Eyepiece
Tripod

ZOOM LENS. Most cameras today come with zoom lenses. They are not essential, but can make focusing easier.

- A TRIPOD. Get as sturdy a tripod as you can afford. This is not a good place to save money. Your animation work requires that your camera stay perfectly steady. A wobbly tripod will produce a wobbly film.

- LIGHTS. You will probably not be able to do all your filming outside during bright, sunny days. You will therefore have to find or buy some strong lights on stands. For your animation work two gooseneck lamps fitted with photoflood bulbs will give you all the light you need.

- FILM. Both Kodachrome 40 and Ektachrome 160 are good color films for the kinds of movies you'll be making. Kodachrome 40 gives you higher quality pictures, but requires brighter lights for indoor filming.

If a manual came with your camera, read it thoroughly. It contains lots of valuable information. Also, don't be afraid to ask people at your local camera store about how your camera works. These people are experts and will be happy to share their knowledge with you.

Finally, get to know your camera by shooting a roll or two of film. Experiment with close-up shots, zooms, stop-frame animation, and different kinds of lighting. Find out just what your camera can and cannot do. Practice now will pay off later in savings of time and money.

At this time it might also be a good idea to select a spot in which to set up your studio. You'll need a place where you can do animation filming, construct miniature sets and characters, do editing, and maybe some sound recording.

The most essential items are a table or desk, chair, and good, strong lighting because you'll need a place to draw your pictures, make out your storyboards, and do some filming.

You will also need something to store materials in. A set of cardboard boxes of varying sizes will probably be easiest to obtain. The boxes will be useful for holding parts of your miniature sets, old sketches, pieces of film, costumes, or other props you may use in your movies.

Put the table or desk and boxes in a clean, well-lighted area. Perhaps your parents will let you use a section of the garage, or maybe you can clear out a corner of your room. Wherever you end up make sure you keep your studio clean and neat. There is nothing more frustrating than not being able to find a prop or piece of equipment because it was mislaid.

As a final touch make everything official with a sign on the door or above your desk. Something like this will let everyone know you're in business—and will keep brothers and sisters away from your equipment and supplies as well:

Official Headquarters

BECKY'S (Your Name)

MONSTER MOVIE STUDIO

Filming Underway On Yet Another Hideous Production

Keep Out!
TRESPASSERS WILL BE EATEN BY OUR LATEST STAR, A TEN-FOOT LIZARD WITH PURPLE EYES AND RAZOR-SHARP TEETH!

WORKING WITH A CAMERA

Simple Monster Movies That Mix Live Action And Animation

One of the most common special effects in use today is the combining of live action with animation. The easiest way to achieve this mix is to draw directly onto the film after the live-action scenes have been filmed and developed. You have probably seen this type of effect in many science fiction and horror films. Usually such things as laser blasts, meteors exploding in space, and ghosts dancing about graveyards are nothing more than skillful drawings sketched onto the live action filmed earlier. Do you remember the laser blasts that came shooting out of the walking tanks in *Return of the Jedi*? Those streaks of fire were sketched onto the finished film. During actual filming of the walking tank miniatures, nothing at all came out of their gun barrels.

Achieving these kinds of effects are surprisingly simple. Here's what you'll need to do it yourself:

- SUPER-8 CAMERA

- LIGHT METER (If your camera doesn't have one built into it)

- PELIKAN-T INKS of the colors you'll need for your effects.

- FINE-TIP PEN for drawing onto the film

As always, you will want to carefully plan out every step of the film before you begin shooting.

Poor planning not only wastes time during production, it often leads to sloppy films.

Think about the kind of story you want to shoot. Do you have an idea for a short, two- or three-minute science fiction or monster movie that mixes live action and animation?

Attack Of The Killer Dots!

A boy is seen running across an open field. Suddenly, tiny purple or red dots come out of the sky and begin attacking him. A friend is nearby, spraying her garden with a hose. The friend turns her hose on the dots, and they are driven away.

Here's How To Do It:

First, shoot your actor running across an open field. Make him run as if he is being pursued by a swarm of dots. Have him run up to a friend. Make sure the friend also "sees" the dots and then have her squirt above your actor with the hose. Send the film out to be developed professionally. After it comes back from the lab, animate the dots using the skills you learned earlier when drawing directly on film.

The Haunted Mansion

A boy and girl are sitting outside a large house. They hear a sound and turn around. The door opens, but nobody comes out. They get up to investigate. Just then, a ghostly white blob comes floating out the door. The kids scream and run off down the street with the ghost in close pursuit.

Here's How To Do It:

Shoot the kids first using the method in *Attack Of The Killer Dots*. After the film has been developed, use white Pelikan-T ink to draw in and animate the ghost.

The Man With The Death-Ray Eyes

A stranger from outer space comes walking down the street. Every time he passes someone, he looks at them with his death-ray eyes. Red beams flash out from his eyes and zap his victims dead. Just as he is about to fry his final victim, a young girl, she picks up a garbage can lid. The death ray bounces off the lid. The girl advances and the man runs away.

Shooting "The Man With The Death-Ray Eyes."
Chad Morgan "zapping" Peter Worth as crew looks on.
After the film has been developed, red streaks will be
drawn onto the film flashing from the alien's eyes to the victim.

Here's How To Do It:

Shoot your actor, dressed in a space suit costume, walking down the street, staring intently and
evilly at the people he passes by. After the film has
been developed and returned from the lab, use red
or pink Pelikan-T ink to draw in the death rays
flashing from the man's eyes onto his victims. Remember to tell your actors that they must pretend

43

they are being toasted by the death rays, whenever the stranger looks at them—there are no rays until you draw them in after the live-action part of the film has been developed.

The Purple Blob

A group of kids discovers a tiny blob of purple goo in the corner of their yard. As they watch in horror, the blob begins to grow, and grow, and grow. Slowly everything begins to disappear and the whole picture is nothing but purple.

Here's How To Do It:

Shoot the kids finding an imaginary piece of purple goo. Then have them watch in horror, perhaps run toward a corner of the yard, as the "goo" spreads. After the film has been developed, use purple Pelikan-T ink to gradually paint in the frames of the film. A nice touch for an ending might be to have a close-up of one of the kids holding up a sign saying "The End." At the end, the sign itself would be covered by the purple blob.

BASIC FILM SHOTS

These are the three basic shots in movie making. They each play an important role in telling your story.

- LONG SHOT. The long shot gives the viewer an over-all picture of the scene. It shows where everything is located. It is most useful when you open a scene or when you have to include a lot of characters or action.

Long shot

- MEDIUM SHOT. The medium shot helps the viewer focus on something important, but still allows the filmmaker to include another character or important piece of scenery. The medium shot is the most common shot seen in movies.

Medium shot

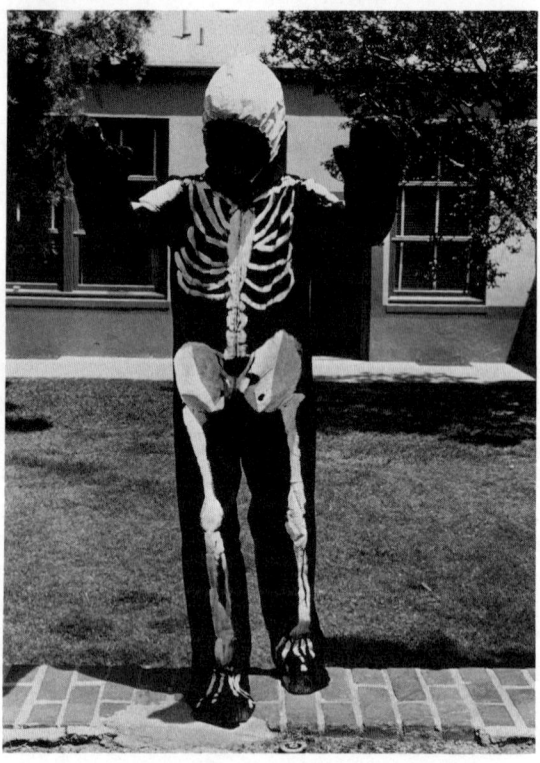

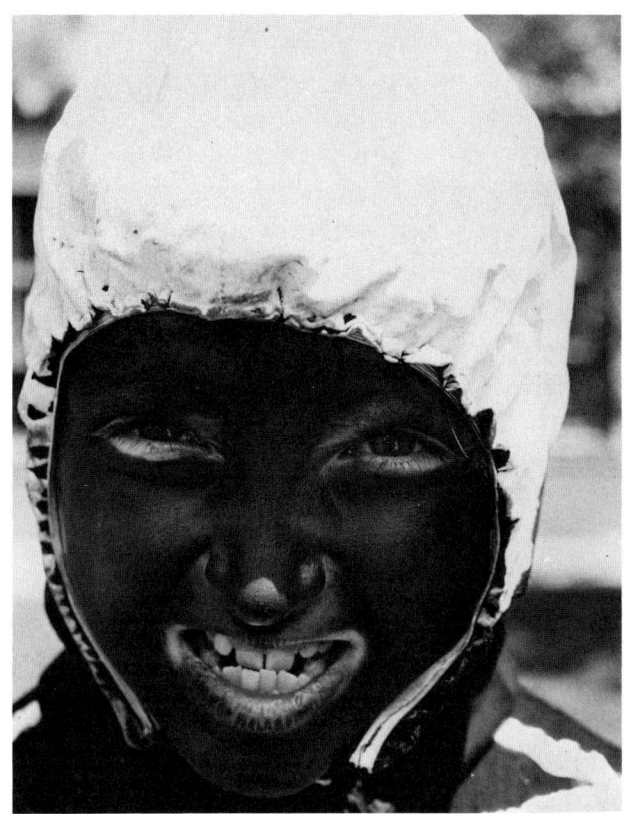

Close-up of Dieter Mattison in full makeup.

- CLOSE-UP. The close-up forces the viewer to look at exactly what you want him to see. Close-ups carry a lot of impact if used correctly. They are useful for showing important details like a character's fangs or an important clue like a bloody spot on the floor.

MAKING THE LIVE FILM—THE DETAILS

Once you have your plot (one you made up, or one of the above), gather together any props (such as a garbage can lid or hose), costumes and equipment (cameras, tripods, lights) that you'll need for the film.

Next, make a storyboard of the action. Each scene in the film will require a separate frame in the storyboard. A sample storyboard for *Attack Of The Killer Dots* might look like the one on the following pages.

1) Titles

2) Dan in field
   (long shot).

3) Dots appear
   (medium shot).

4) Dots chase Dan
   (medium shot).

5) Dan sees Ann watering
   flowers (medium shot).

6) Dan points to dots
   (medium shot).

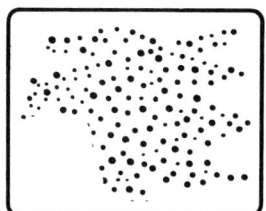

7) Close-up of dots.

8) Dots attack Ann and Dan (medium shot).

9) Ann squirts dots with water (medium shot).

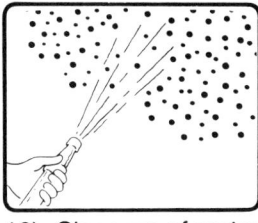

10) Close-up of water hitting dots (close-up).

11) Dots begin to flee from water (medium shot).

12) Dan and Ann shake hands (medium shot).

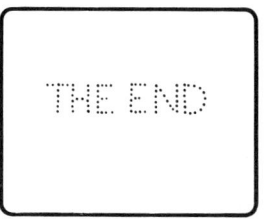

13) End titles

When you have completed your storyboard, check it over to make sure all the scenes have been included. Show it to friends and ask them if they understand the plot. They should be able to. If you have included any unnecessary scenes, anything that doesn't advance your story, cut them out. They will only detract from your film. Once again, remember to keep everything as simple as possible.

THE OPENING CREDITS

Before you start shooting you need to consider the beginning of your film, the opening credits. Titles often set the mood for a film. Sloppy credits at the beginning of a film often announce the coming of a sloppy film. Well-thought-out, creative titles, on the other hand, can draw in your audience and gain their immediate interest in what is to follow.

Give some thought to the kind of titles you want. For a film like *Attack Of The Killer Dots* you might want to spell out the titles in dots. You can even animate the dots if you wish. Simply photograph the title board, click off two frames, add some dots, click off two more frames, and so on until the title is formed. When projected, the title will seem to spell itself out before the viewer's eyes.

Other titles should contain your name as the filmmaker and the names of your actors, actresses, and assistants. Your friends have worked hard to help you make your movie. Give them credit in the titles. It's a nice way to say thanks.

Don't forget to leave room for your "The End" title. Again, try to make it as interesting as possible. Animate it perhaps, or have a character hold up a sign saying "The End." First impressions are important, but last impressions are what people remember longest. Make sure your audience goes away with a positive feeling for your film.

SHOOTING THE FILM

On the day of the shooting, assemble all your equipment and actors at the location where you will be filming. Rehearse each scene before filming. Go over the storyboard with your actors. Make certain they understand that they will not actually be seeing any dots or ghosts. But be sure they know where the dots or ghosts are supposed to appear, so that they know in which direction to run or stare. This is called "blocking" the scene or action. Your players must pretend to see the monstrous sights that you will draw in later, so that when the effects do appear on the film, it will look realistic.

During the rehearsal, look through the camera to see how the scene will look on film. Do the actors and actresses stay in the frame? Is there always plenty of room to fit in the drawings?

It's a good idea to rehearse before you begin filming.

Focus

A fuzzy picture is very difficult to look at, so you want to make sure that each shot is in focus. Reflex-type cameras have viewfinders that see directly through the lens. Therefore, what you see in the viewfinder is what you will see when the film is developed. To focus a reflex camera, simply twist the lens while looking through the viewfinder till you get a clean, crisp picture.

If the camera is not equipped for reflex viewing, then focus according to how far away your actors are from the lens. You may want to measure the distance (up to twenty feet) with a tape measure, but you should be able to estimate the distance close enough to get a good focus. Once you know the distance, turn the camera lens focus ring to the proper distance. The lens is marked four feet, six feet, ten feet, and so on. Beyond about twenty feet the camera is always in focus at its maximum opening.

Exposure

You want your film to be properly exposed. The only thing worse than a film that is overexposed—pale and anemic—is one that is so underexposed and dark that you can't see a thing. If your camera has an automatic light meter, you won't have to worry about proper exposure. The electric eye on the camera will take care of it.

If you don't have an automatic light meter, you will need to use a hand light meter in order to set your exposure. There is an adjustable opening on the camera lens, called a diaphragm. The diaphragm can be opened wide to let in a lot of light or narrowed to let in less light, and can thus control the amount of exposure. The settings for the diaphragm are called *f-stops* and start at 1.6, which is wide open, and go past 2, 2.8, 4, 5.6, 8, 11, 16, to 22, which is nearly closed. On a bright, sunny day, you will want the camera to "squint" down at 16 or 22. If you are working in the shade, or on a dark, cloudy day, the lens should be more open, in the range of 2.8 or 4.

Light meters need to be set according to your film speed, which for Super-8 is eighteen frames per second. You also need to set the light meter according to your film's ASA rating. The ASA rating tells you how sensitive to light the film is, and is always stated on the box in which you buy your film. Standard color rating for Ektachrome film, for instance, is about 25. This may sound very technical and complicated, but it's not. If you read the instructions that come with your meter, and practice with it before you start shooting, you'll find that getting the proper exposure is not at all difficult.

If you can, shoot your film straight through, in sequence, beginning with your opening credits and finishing with your end titles. It won't be easy to shoot straight through without a mistake, but it's worth a try. If you make no mistakes, you will be able to draw on your film as soon as it comes back from the lab.

So, after your film has been shot and developed, take a good look at it. Are there any mistakes or unnecessary scenes? Has anything been left out? Is everything in focus and properly exposed? If there are any glaring mistakes or omissions, if you find you have to cut out some of the scenes or move others around, you will have to do some re-shooting, editing, or both. (The section on editing begins on page 87.)

Once your film is ready for the drawing to be added, take it to your studio and unwind it a bit at a time onto your desk. Tape down the film and, with Pelikan-T inks, animate in your special effects whether they are dots, ghosts, or purple blobs. Remember, to achieve animation, you must advance the drawing of your dots or ghosts slightly every two frames or so.

As soon as the ink has dried, you can project your film. If you've done everything carefully, you should have produced a bone-chilling, spine-tingling epic that you'll be proud to show, and your friends will be scared witless to see.

SIMPLE SPECIAL EFFECTS

Fade-outs and Fade-ins

Most movies contain a number of fade-outs (where the scene slowly goes dark) and fade-ins (where the light increases till we can see the scene). Usually these effects are done in a laboratory. But you can do them just as easily in the camera.

If you are animating a scene, you can easily fade it in or out by adjusting the light as you film. For instance, if you want to fade in a scene, you simply begin filming in very dim light. Before you begin *filming* either dim your lights with a dimmer, or simply move the lights away from your artwork. Click off two to four frames and either turn up the lights or move them closer. Do this three or four times till you are at the proper light level. To fade out a scene, just turn down the lights (or move them away) every few frames until the scene is too dark to see.

If you are filming live action, your fade-in or fade-out can be done by adjusting your exposure. For instance, you may wish to fade in on a creature emerging from a swamp. All you have to do is start with the diaphragm of the lens closed all the way down. Then, with the camera focused on the monster, have an assistant slowly open the diaphragm of the lens past f-stops 16, 11, and onto 8 or 5.6, wherever the creature is plainly visible. To fade out a scene simply have the assistant close down the lens while the camera is shooting the scene.

Be careful that the assistant does not get a hand in front of the lens!

Slow Motion

For slow motion all you have to do is speed up your camera, if you have one capable of this. If, for instance, you want to show your creature falling into the mud excruciatingly slowly, instead of running your camera at the normal 18 frames per second, turn it up to 56 frames per second. When the film is shown, the action will appear to be in slow motion.

Speeded-Up Motion

When you film a scene at a speed slower than the normal 18 frames per second, the action will appear to be speeded up. Perhaps you've seen some of the early Charlie Chaplin and Keystone Kops comedy films where everyone is running around at double speed. These types of action can be duplicated by filming scenes at anywhere from six to twelve frames per second.

A
HOME FOR
HORRIBLE
CREATURES

Creating Miniature Sets And
Models

In this chapter let's look at how you can put together inexpensive monster movie sets and models to make stop-frame animation movies. Stop-frame animation, which involves the use of miniature sets, models, and characters, is like regular animation except that instead of photographing a drawing, you photograph a miniature model in a miniature set. And instead of changing the drawing slightly every two frames, you move your model slightly, take two more frames, then move it again, and so on.

Hollywood's monsters have been stop-frame-animated models for more than 70 years. King Kong was an animated model in some scenes, so were the Ton-tons, the kangaroolike horses in *The Empire Strikes Back*, and so was Pegasus in *Clash of the Titans*.

What kind of movie are you going to make? Will it be a creature feature set in a prehistoric jungle? Will it be an outer-space adventure set on a cold, icy planet? Or did you have in mind a monster epic starring a twenty-foot lizard on the rampage?

Whatever kind of film you decide on, you will need to construct or obtain miniature models and sets. For instance, for a jungle picture you will need to draw or build a small jungle as well as make or buy dinosaur models. Outer-space movies will re-

A papier-mâché volcano adds a realistic touch to a prehistoric setting.

quire rocket ships and background paintings of stars. If you wish to have a giant monster destroy a city, you're going to need a miniature metropolis for your beast to squash.

Start by making a list of all the sets, props, creatures, and backgrounds you'll need for your film. As always, try to keep things as simple as possible.

Once your list is complete, look around your house. You may already have many of the things you need. Perhaps you've got a toy dinosaur or wind-up robot that's just been itching to get into the movies. Can you find a photograph of a galaxy

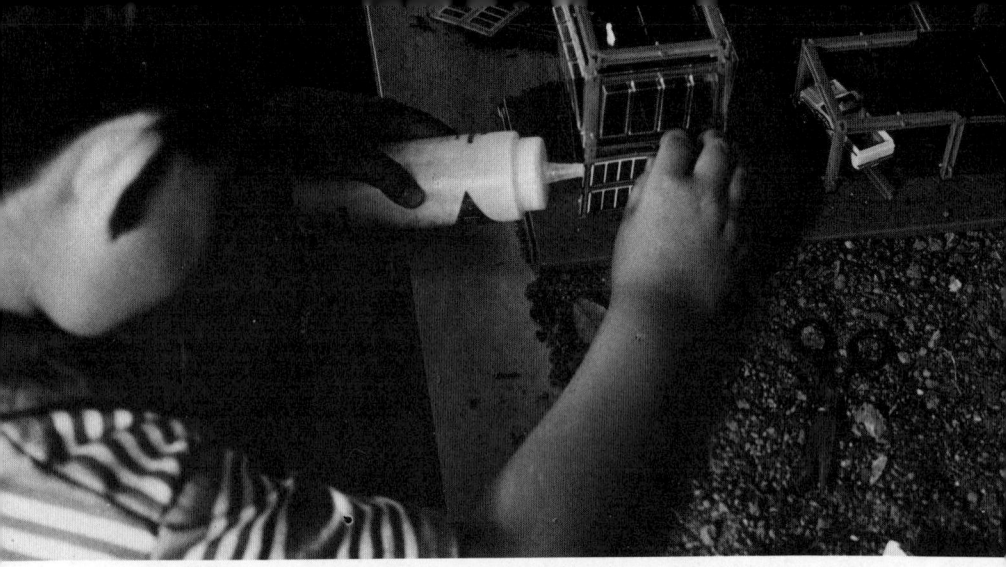

Some toy stores sell kits that you make into towns
and cities. All you need do is assemble and glue.

in an old magazine that can be used as a background for your space adventure? Do you have a
dollhouse that was about to go into the trash? Don't
toss it out. Instead, let a monster rip it apart in
your next movie.

If you don't have the props you need, ask your
friends if they have any toys or pictures you can
borrow. Whatever you don't have or can't borrow,
you will have to buy at a toy store or, better yet,
build it yourself.

- A lush jungle can be made by collecting
  branches from trees and sticking them into the
  ground. A sheet of green paper covered with
  fresh leaves glued to the surface makes an excellent background.

- A black sheet of paper painted with stars and planets can serve as a background for your outer-space movie. Rocky asteroids can be easily made by wadding up colored paper. Hang the paper by black thread in front of the background. Bottle caps and buttons, touched up with poster paint, also make interesting outer-space objects to either glue to the background or hang in front.

- If you're going to set your rocket ship down on an alien planet, you'll have to build an appropriate set. A light-colored sheet of paper decorated with a few clouds will serve well for a sky. Since this is an alien planet, you can make the sky any color you like. Or, if possible, find a picture of the sky that you can cut from a magazine and paste it down on the construction paper. It might be best to set your scene up outside. If your planet is a dry, desertlike place, put your characters in a sandbox. If it is cold and icy, use soapflakes or baking soda to simulate snow. Tin cans of various sizes, painted with poster paints, work well as futuristic buildings on your planet's surface.

More down-to-earth cities can be built out of milk cartons of various sizes: half-gallon cartons for skyscrapers and pint cartons for houses. Paint in windows and doors or cut out pictures of houses and buildings and glue them to the cartons with rubber cement.

Cardboard boxes can be transformed into a block
of buildings with scissors and paint, as
Walter Hsieh does here.

Eighth-inch-thick wooden dowels (round sticks),
painted with black or brown and strung with black
thread make excellent telephone poles. Fill your
streets with toy cars and miniature people. Most
large toy stores sell inexpensive bags of tiny figures
such as toy animals, soldiers, and cowboys. A little
dab of poster paint can change most of these figures
to the shoppers and workers you need for your city.
You will probably want to leave the soldiers as they
are. They'll be needed to battle your monster when
he launches his attack on your milk-carton metropolis.

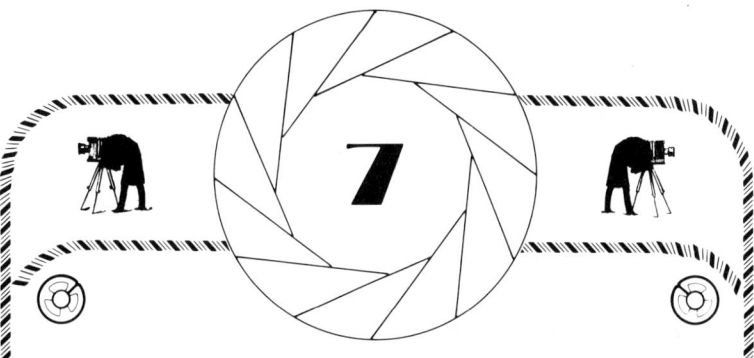

CREATING
MONSTERS
FOR YOUR
MOVIES

Now that your set is complete, you need to bring it to life with a thoroughly repulsive monster or two.

USING A TOY

The easiest character to cast is one that has already been made—a toy. If you elect to use a toy monster in your miniature set, pick a creature that is easy to manipulate. The kind of stop-action movie you will be making will require your main character to be moved by hand every two to four frames. The easier the model is to move the faster your filming will go. Most toy stores carry three- to five-inch-tall rubberized monsters with flexible arms and legs. Toy manufacturers also turn out detailed plastic kits of famous monsters from King Kong to Darth Vader. The legs and arms of these kit monsters are often hinged, allowing you to move them in a highly realistic way.

USING CUT-OUTS

Another easy way to make a stop-action film is with cut-out characters. Your cut-out character is laid flat against a two-dimensional background. Instead of peering into the set from the side, your camera is above, looking down on your animation

Toys with flexible arms and legs are easiest to work with.

table. With everything flat, filming, as well as ma-nipulation of the characters, is simple. You can either draw your monstrous movie star or you can cut out a picture of him or her from a favorite monster magazine or comic book. Cut out a side view, a front view, and close-up of the face of your monster if these pictures are available.

After he, she, it has been cut out, glue the charac-ter onto a piece of cardboard.

Mae Lin shooting a scene using cut-out characters.

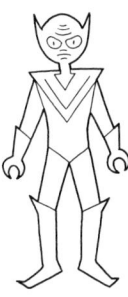

1) Glue your cut-out monster to a piece of cardboard cut to its shape.

2) Separate the arms and legs from the body—carefully!

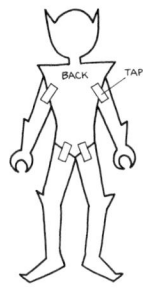

BACK   TAPE

3) Turn your monster over, and tape the arms and legs back on.

4) The tape will keep the limbs on, but allows you to move his arms and legs to different positions.

Cut the figure out of the cardboard. Cut the figure again at the top of the legs and the shoulders with a sharp knife, so that the arms and the legs are separate. An adult should help you with this stage.

Hinge the arms and legs back onto the character using strong packing tape on the back of the cardboard.

Now you have a character that can be easily moved across your set.

CREATING CLAY CHARACTERS

Since stop-frame animation requires that your characters be moved often, you want main characters that are flexible. You need monsters who can realistically turn their heads, lift up their feet, or raise their arms. For these conditions clay characters are not only the most flexible, but the most realistic as well.

Scott Hunter creating clay characters to star in a forthcoming outer-space epic.

Make sure your clay character is the right size so that he looks natural among the rest of your props.

Make your characters out of modeling clay, which is available in most toy stores. Be sure to select a soft clay. It will be the easiest to work with. Also check that you can paint on it, if you decide to.

As you create your characters keep in mind that your clay figure has to be the right size. If your figure is supposed to ride in a spaceship, you can't make him so big he won't fit inside the rocket. At the same time you don't want to create a character that will be so small he'd be difficult to photograph.

As you work, remind yourself to keep things simple. A nice ball of clay for a body, a round head with holes for eyes and a slit for a mouth, and pipe cleaners wrapped with clay and stuck into the body for arms and legs, will make a fine creature. You may also wish to paint on features and clothes. Use doll's hair for a wig or beard.

Of course, your main character doesn't have to be made of clay, or cut from a book. If you'd rather star a favorite doll or wind-up toy, or make something completely different, then do so. You're the casting director. It is your film. Feel free to experiment at any stage of the filmmaking process. It is a good way to learn what works and what does not.

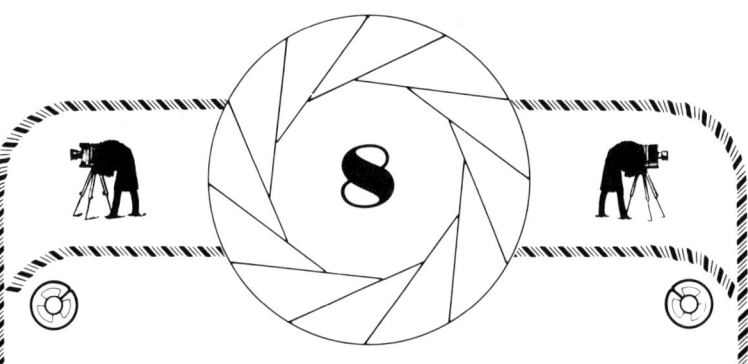

STOP-FRAME
ANIMATION
IN YOUR
MINIATURE SET

Bringing Your Characters To
Life

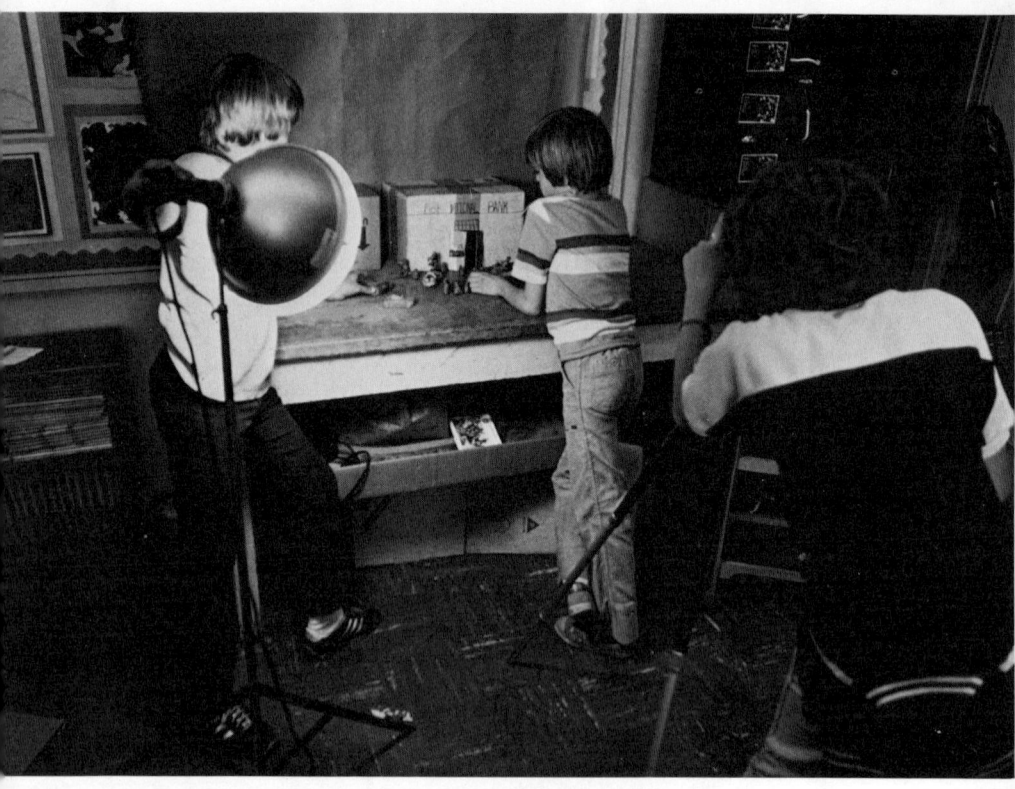

Using a floodlight to light your miniature set.

You are ready to begin filming your monster movie classic! You have already:

- Sketched out a storyboard that shows all the scenes you wish to shoot.

- Created your miniature set and gathered together your characters.

- Set up your camera, tripod, light meter, film, and lights.

- Arranged everything indoors on a low table well lighted by the sun, or with photoflood lights, or you have set it up outside in the sun.

To save yourself from editing the film later, consider beginning your filming with the opening titles. As discussed earlier, your titles can take many forms. They can be still shots or animated. Try to tie them in with the theme of your movie. Make them as good as possible. You want your film to get off to a good start.

Once you've filmed your titles you can move right into your story. It is best to open your film with an *establishing shot*. Establishing shots, in fact, open almost all films. Basically they are nothing more than a long shot of the opening scene. If the first scene takes place in a swamp, the opening shot should probably be a bird's-eye view of mud flats and twisted trees. Then the camera might move down through the trees into the swamp. Finally it would settle on our star, a half-man, half-crocodile creature as he emerges from a murky pool of water. To have opened the movie with a close-up of the creature's head may have been shocking, but it would also have been confusing. It is important that your audience knows where the action is taking place. So open with a wide overview of the scene.

ANIMATING TWO-DIMENSIONAL CUT-OUT CHARACTERS

Your camera should be positioned on a tripod looking down on your artwork. The artwork and cut-out characters can be laid flat under the camera, either on a table top or on the floor. Your tripod must be solidly positioned. You don't want it to move. Use a light meter to determine the opening of your camera lens. Set your focus and you are ready to begin filming.

After your establishing shot you may wish to pan over to your main character. *Pan* means to move across the scene. If you are shooting the swamp scene, you may want to pan across the treetops till you reach the swamp creature.

In a live-action movie the camera moves to show us the scene. In stop-frame animation the background moves and the camera stays in the same place. In order to pan across the treetops, you need to click off two to four frames of film and then move the scene under the camera about one-quarter of an inch. Then click off a few more frames until you have arrived at the murky pool which holds the monster. You can pan as far as you want, but about 12–18 inches of artwork passing beneath your camera will probably be enough to solidly establish your setting. Be sure that your background and your cut-outs are taped down between shots. If you accidentally move them, or a breeze blows them off the table, you might not remember where they were on your set, and you would have to start all over.

Before you animate your cut-out characters, study how you—or your dog or cat—move. Notice how one foot comes up, an arm swings forward, another foot comes up, and so on. Animate your cut-outs in the same way. Their hinged arms and legs make them easy to move across the scene. Pick up a foot and move it one-quarter of an inch. At the same time, swing an arm forward one-quarter of an inch. Then click off two to four frames. After each quarter-inch movement, take two to four frames until the action is complete. If you want your character to turn, you are going to need a side view of him or her in addition to the front view. Using a side, front, and, if possible, a back view of your characters, you can have them do anything your script calls for.

If you wish to have your characters speak, make three separate mouths for their faces. One mouth is closed, one is half open, and the third is open all the way.

Film two frames with the mouth closed. Lift off the closed mouth and replace it with the mouth that is half open and shoot two more frames. Then

Three interchangeable mouths make it possible for your character to speak.

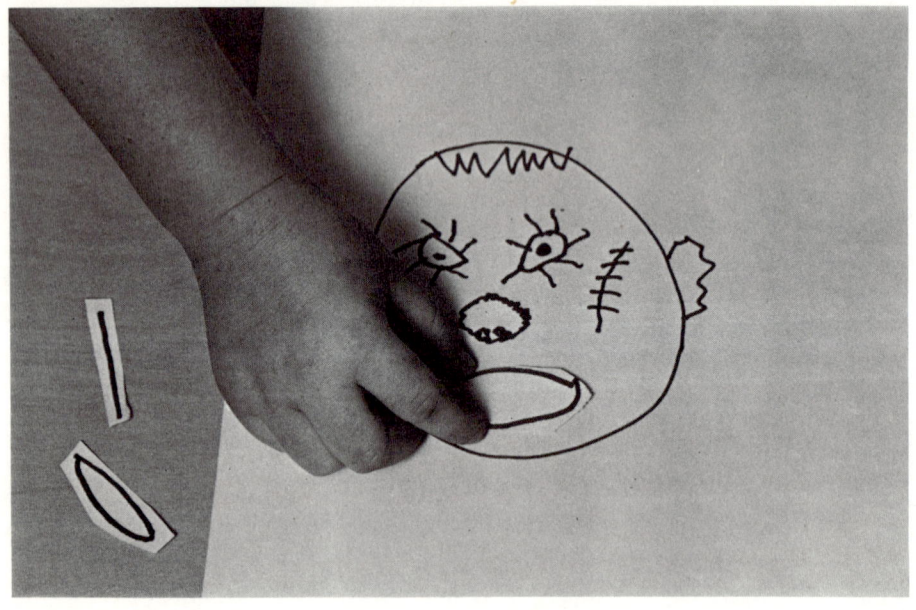

film two frames with the mouth wide open. To close the mouth you must reverse the process.

A good rule of thumb to follow is that you can get in two words every time the mouth opens and closes. Long speeches can take you days to film, so keep dialogue to a minimum. Replaceable parts also work well for eyes and eyebrows. As long as you're moving a mouth you might as well alternate eyes as well. If each eye has an eyeball which is positioned slightly to the left (the character seems to be looking left), you can make the eyes appear to shift by moving *both* eyeballs toward the right. The character will appear to be looking from one side to the other. This is a good effect if not overdone. Be sure to move the eyeballs in the same direction at the same time; otherwise your character will squint!

After you have made two or three films you will have a better feel for how best to move your cut-out characters. Perhaps you may want to slow down the action by clicking off more than four frames between movements, perhaps you may want to speed it up by clicking off less. Experiment. You shouldn't expect your first film to be a masterpiece. If you can learn from your mistakes, your second film will be even better, and by your third film you'll be making movies good enough to earn an Academy Award for Scary Short Subjects.

ANIMATING THREE-DIMENSIONAL CHARACTERS

When working with three-dimensional characters and three-dimensional sets, it is generally easier to shoot horizontally at the set instead of down on it from above. Again, establish the proper exposure and focus, and securely anchor your tripod before you begin filming.

Click off two to four frames . . .

Move your characters slightly. Click off two to four more frames
each time, until the action is complete.

Your clay and toy characters can be moved in the same way as cut-outs. Move their arms, legs, tails, and heads slightly (about one-quarter inch) each time you click off two to four frames. The big advantage of three-dimensional characters is that they look realistic. They are easy to turn, and they move naturally about your three-dimensional miniature set. If you wish your characters to speak, scream, or moan, you can easily move the mouths of clay characters. Toy characters do not usually have movable mouths, so when these characters speak, make sure the audience doesn't see their mouths. Have their backs turned or focus on something else.

As with the cut-out figures you must be careful not to bump or move your set between shots. But clay and toy characters can't usually be taped down between shots. So take special care during your three-dimensional filming.

Because you are working with miniature sets and models, your camera will always be close to the subject, only about eighteen inches away. Most close-up camera lenses are only able to keep a small part of the scene in focus. Backgrounds will usually be slightly hazy. Keep this in mind when filming. Make certain the *action* is always in focus. If your main character is involved in the action, focus on him. If the action is taking place in the background, focus on that and let everything else get a little hazy.

With miniatures, models, and stop-action animation you can tell almost any story you can dredge from the depths of your monstrous mind. To help you get started here are some sample story beginnings. You'll have to come up with the appropriately horrible endings.

Revenge Of The Swamp Creature

A dinosaur is slowly lumbering through a swamp. It pauses to drink from a small pool. A scaly alligator-headed creature rises up out of the pool. It climbs from the pool and begins chasing the dinosaur through the swamp.

Planet Of The Sand Monsters

A spaceship lands on a sandy planet (a sandbox with a pink cardboard sheet representing the sky). Two astronauts descend from the ship. They walk to a small hill. Suddenly, three hideous creatures pop out of the sand. The astronauts turn to face the creatures.

Attack Of The Hundred-Foot Man

It is twelve noon and the streets of the city are full of pedestrians and cars. A huge monster, as tall as a ten-story building, appears at the end of the street. He begins walking down the street, crushing cars and pulling over buildings as he goes. The people run away in panic. At the end of the street they decide to try and lead the monster over to a deep hole at a construction site. Will they be successful in luring him into the trap? Only you know for sure.

CREATING THE WOLFMAN . . . AND OTHERS

Combining Live Action With Stop-Frame Animation

If you don't think you have the patience to make a whole movie using stop-frame animation, or if you can't spend the time building miniature sets and models, don't despair. You can still make monster movies.

What you can do is make a live-action movie that mixes in a bit of stop-frame animation. The technique of mixing the two has been used successfully in countless science fiction and monster movies. It is the trick that allowed us to watch the kindly Dr. Jekyll turn into the grotesque Mr. Hyde. It is the process that turned Dracula into a bat before our very eyes, and it's the trick that made an ordinary man change into the Wolfman—his teeth turning to fangs, his nose to a snout, and hair growing on his hands and face. I think you'll find these kinds of movies easy to make, and fun, too.

The early stages of production, whether you're doing animation or live action, are the same.

- You need a script.

- You need to make a storyboard.

- You need to gather together your equipment.

- You need to assemble your cast of characters and costume them appropriately.

- You need to locate the proper setting in which to film your movie.

Once you settle on an idea for your live-action film, you will need to find appropriate costumes for your human actors. Are you going to do a picture about a wolfman? Frankenstein's monster? Invaders from space? Each of these subjects requires different kinds of costumes. Your library can offer you a wide variety of books on easy-to-make costumes, or check your closets for old Halloween outfits.

After you have clothed your cast in their monstrous garb, you must direct them—show them how to act. Robots walk stiffly and mechanically; a wolf creature will shuffle along like the half animal he is; you may want your bug-eyed beast from outer space to hop about like a rabbit or slither along like a snake. Give your characters personalities. It will make them all the more real and therefore all the more frightening to your audience.

Setting is as important as costuming to the success of your live-action movie. Pick your locations carefully. Whether you select a dark forest to stage your wolfman epic, a run-down house for your ghost story, or a desolate desert for your Planet X science fiction adventure, you may need to get permission to film from the owner of the property.

Most people are more than willing to turn their land or home into a movie set as long as you ask them first and promise to put everything back in order once you leave. Professional filmmakers usually get permission in writing, and you may wish to do this also. All you need is a simple sheet of paper stating that you take responsibility for anything that happens in connection with the filming, that you will clean up afterwards, and stating the dates on which you wish to film. The paper should be signed by both you and the property owner.

Look around your neighborhood or town for good monster settings. If you have in mind an outer-space epic that takes place on a sandy planet, make certain you know where there is a stretch of sand dunes or a wide beach for your filming. If you can't find such a setting, you will have to come up with another idea. Sometimes, however, a setting can give you an idea for a film. If there is an old, run-down house in your area that looks as if it might be haunted, and you can get permission to film there, then you might try to write a movie that uses the house as a setting.

Here are some suggestions for making live-action movies that combine with stop-frame animation. You may just want to use part of one of these suggested stories. Or you can make up your own.

Invasion Of The Droids

A birthday party is going on when suddenly the door bursts open, and in walk some creatures from another planet (in appropriate outer-space outfits)—the Droids. Somebody picks up a glass and is about to throw it at the Droids, when one of the aliens points a silver wand at the glass. All at once the glass disappears. The wand is pointed at other objects, and they disappear, too. The alien begins pointing the wand at the partygoers. One by one they disappear till only one girl is left. She grabs the wand out of the Droid's hand and points it at him and his friends. They disappear. The girl is all alone. Then she accidentally points the wand at her reflection in a mirror. Poof! She's gone, too. The final shot is of the wand lying on the floor of the empty room.

How You Shoot It:

Invasion of The Droids involves one of the simplest stop-frame tricks in filmmaking. All you do to make the object disappear is to have everyone freeze the second the wand is pointed at something. At that same moment you stop the camera, which must be stationary on a tripod. Then you (or an assistant) walk onto the set and remove the object, such as the glass from the frozen, upraised hand of your actor. You start the camera again, and the actors resume their movements. The only difference in the scene is that the glass has somehow magically disappeared.

A "droid" points his "disappearing wand" at the unsuspecting victim, Heather.

Stop the camera. Two of the actors freeze while Heather walks out of the picture.

Start the camera. On film,
it seems that Heather has
vanished into thin air.

It is very important that no one moves once the camera has been turned off. An exception, of course, is when a person is being made invisible. In that case, as soon as the camera is off, that person walks off the set. When the camera is back on, the other actors should look with surprise and fright at the empty spot where their friend once stood.

Attack Of The Zombies

This film begins at the gates of a graveyard. Two or three "zombies" (people dressed in tattered clothes with smudged faces and rumpled hair, looking as if they'd just crawled from the grave) walk down the street. They walk up to a person and touch him. At once that person begins to turn into a zombie, too. A scar grows on his face. His hair becomes rumpled and he develops a sunken-eyed, deathly look. Then he joins the original zombies and walks off down the street with them. The zombies do this transformation three or four times. Finally some kids throw a bunch of banana peels on the sidewalk. The zombies slip and fall, hit their heads, and are all knocked out. The kids congratulate each other on their victory.

How You Shoot It:

The only special effects trick needed for this film is the changing of the normal person into a zombie after he has been touched. As in the previous film, you must stop the camera and have everyone freeze the moment the person's face has been touched. While your actors and actresses remain frozen, move in and apply makeup to his face. After you have put on a little makeup, shoot four to eight frames. Move back in and apply some more makeup. Try to shoot at least 60 frames, six to eight frames at a time, during the transformation of the person into the zombie. Once the transformation is complete movement can resume. If you prefer, you don't have to have the zombies actually touch their victims. You can have them zap the people with death rays from their eyes. The rays, of course, will be drawn directly onto the film by you after the movie has been developed.

Birth Of The Wolfman

In this short film a mother buys her son a chemistry set. He takes it into his room and mixes together some chemicals. He drinks the potion and begins to change into a wolfman. Hair grows on his face. He sprouts fangs. When the transformation is complete, he looks at himself in the mirror and smiles. Then he mixes up a new concoction and drinks it down. As we watch, he sheds his hairy wolfman guise and returns to the boy he was. At the end his mother comes into the room. "Did you make anything?" she asks.

"Nothing much," he says and smiles. "Nothing much at all."

How You Shoot It:

This movie is made the same way we made the last film. After your actor has drunk the potion, have him freeze. Then move in and begin to apply makeup to his face. Fake hair can be made from a type of yarn called "roving wool." It's available at knitting supply stores. Apply it in tufts to your character's face with spirit gum. Parts of the face not covered with hair can be blacked in with black eye shadow.

Every time you apply a little more hair or makeup, step back and click off four to eight frames of film. Your wolfman must remain stationary during the transformation to ensure a smooth transformation on the film. Also, don't forget to keep the camera still as well.

When you shoot your wolfman turning back into a boy or girl, simply reverse the process. Remove a tuft of hair, and shoot a few frames, and so on.

These are just three ideas for combining live-action with stop-frame animation. You should be able to think of many more. Perhaps you'll come up with a horrific story so scary you'll frighten yourself. Let's hope so.

POLISHING YOUR FILM

Editing And Sound Recording

SIMPLE EDITING

If you have been lucky—very lucky—you won't need to edit your monster movie. You will have shot your titles first, shot the scenes in order, and finally shot your end titles at the end, all without once making a mistake. Chances are, however, you did make a mistake or two. Or perhaps you want to add a scene you forgot to include. Or maybe there is a shot you want to take out. If so, you will have to edit your film. For simple editing you will need:

- A PROJECTOR
- AN EDITOR-VIEWER (not absolutely essential, but nice to have)
- A SPLICER
- TWO REELS (one to hold the film and one to take it up after it goes through the editor-viewer)
- A GREASE PENCIL
- SPLICING TAPE OR GLUE
- A TABLE OR DESK

Before you cut your first piece of film, look at your movie on the screen or on an editor-viewer. An editor-viewer is a small desktop machine with a small screen on top. The film is fed through the viewer and hand cranked in front of the screen. With a viewer you can stop on any one frame and then

Jennifer Lewis sets up her film on an editor-viewer.

mark the frame with a grease pencil so you will know where to cut.

As you view the film, make notes about what you want to cut or move. When you are ready to cut your film, put it in the splicer. The splicer will hold your film while you cut it. It will also hold two pieces of film you want to splice together. The two pieces of cut film can be joined together with either glue or splicing tape. Splicing is not at all difficult. An instruction booklet should come with your

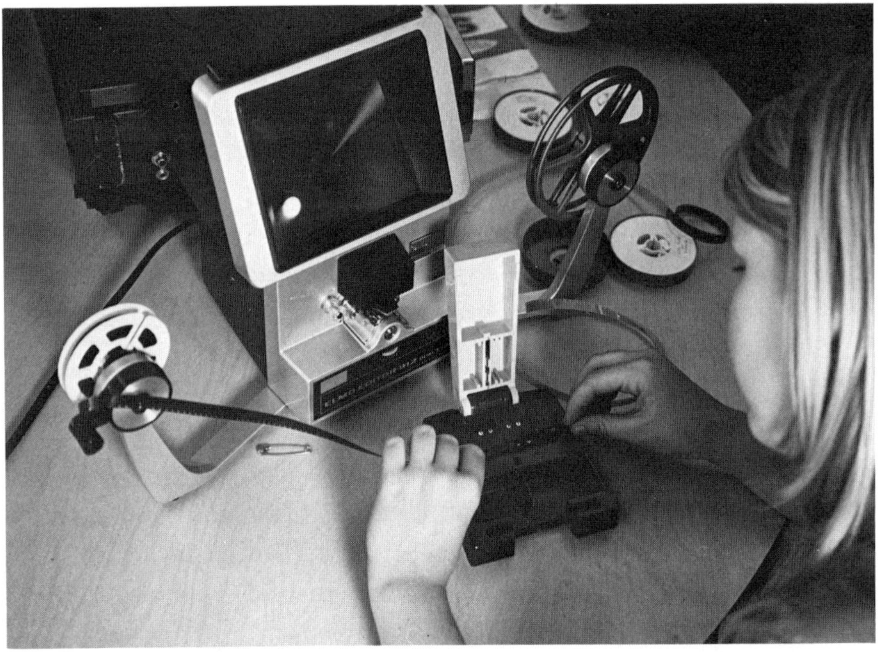

After viewing the film, Jennifer knows what she wants to edit out. The splicer is used to cut out the frames you don't want and then splice your film back together.

splicer. Study it carefully. If you have any questions, ask someone at your local camera store to help you.

Don't be afraid to cut out pieces of your film. Directors normally shoot ten to twenty times more film then they will use in the final movie. If something is not advancing your story, then cut it out. A shot of a beautiful sunset may be very pretty, but if it doesn't fit into the movie, it doesn't belong. It will only distract the audience.

A SIMPLE SOUNDTRACK

Sound is nearly as important as sight in a monster movie. The wolfman is much more frightening when we can hear his howl. The spaceship seems all the more real when we hear the roar of its engines, and we're much more sympathetic to the victim of the Giant Slug when we hear his blood-curdling screams.

If your Super-8 camera is equipped to record live sound, then you are most fortunate. All you need to do to finish your film is to add a little music and a few sound effects to the sound you recorded live while you were shooting your movie.

Most cameras, however, are not equipped to make a live sound recording. Therefore, you will have to add the sound later. The easiest thing to do is to put your sound on a tape recorder, and then play it back each time you project your film.

Start by looking at your finished film a number of times. As you are viewing the movie, make careful notes about the kind of narration, sound effects, and music you will need and where you want it to go.

Next, collect any sound effects or records you will need. Large record stores sell sound effects records. These contain such effects as a raging fire, onrushing trains, rumblings of an earthquake, or the explosion of a bomb. You may want to purchase one or more of these records to use in your film. But, better yet, why not record the sounds yourself on a tape recorder? For instance:

- By crinkling up a ball of stiff cellophane, you can get the sound of a fire.

- By blowing into the top of a large, empty bottle, you get a deep, eerie moan.

- By rattling a piece of stiff cardboard, you get the sound of thunder.

- You can take a tape recorder out near a busy street during rush hour and record the sounds of traffic.

- Turn on a vacuum cleaner, and you've got the roar of a rocket blasting off into space.

- Click a parking meter, and you have a laser gun being cocked. (This is how it was done for the movie *Star Wars*.)

Use your imagination and your ears, and you'll discover all kinds of everyday sounds that will make excellent effects for your movie.

Unless you have a sound camera, you should probably not try to synchronize the voices of the actors with the film of them speaking. Combining film and sound from two different sources (lip-sync) often results in awkward and artificial jumps when the dialogue does not keep pace with the movements of the actors' mouths, or vice versa. In other words, don't try to record voices after the film has been shot as it will be almost impossible to match the voices with the movement of the characters' lips. It is all right to have your characters talking, but make sure that during filming their lips are hidden behind a mask, such as a robot or Darth Vader outfit, or their backs are turned. With animation, you can have direct shots of lips speaking because the movements are so exaggerated.

When you are ready to record your finished soundtrack, assemble your equipment. This should include:

- A projector loaded with the finished film and a screen to show it on.

- Necessary sound effects materials such as cellophane and/or a tape recorder with the sounds prerecorded in the order in which you wish them to play.

- A phonograph with the records you want on the soundtrack.

- Actors and actresses to read narration and to help run the recording and sound effects equipment.

- A tape recorder with a clean roll of tape so that you can record the finished soundtrack.

Recorded and live sound effects are taped in conjunction with showing the film. This will be the soundtrack.

First, rehearse. Run the film through the camera a number of times. Make sure that everyone knows when to read narration, put on the right record, make the right sound effect, or give the proper scream.

Then start the tape recorder and speak the words, "Soundtrack for (name of your movie) ready; begin."

Stop the recorder and start the film. As soon as the first frame of the titles comes on the screen, start the recorder and begin to record your soundtrack as the film plays. This procedure will insure that your tape recorder and film can always be synchronized. In the future all you'll have to do is stop the recorder at the word "begin" and then start it again when you see the first frame of the title, and the film will be in sync.

As the film is being projected, record the sound effects, narration, and music on the recorder. Your friends will need to help you turn the record players and recorders on and off and add the sound at the appropriate time.

After the sound has been recorded, show the film along with your completed, synchronized soundtrack. If it isn't just right, do it again. Nothing can be more distracting than sound that is inappropriate or out of place. A monster movie is supposed to make its audience hysterical with fright, not with laughter.

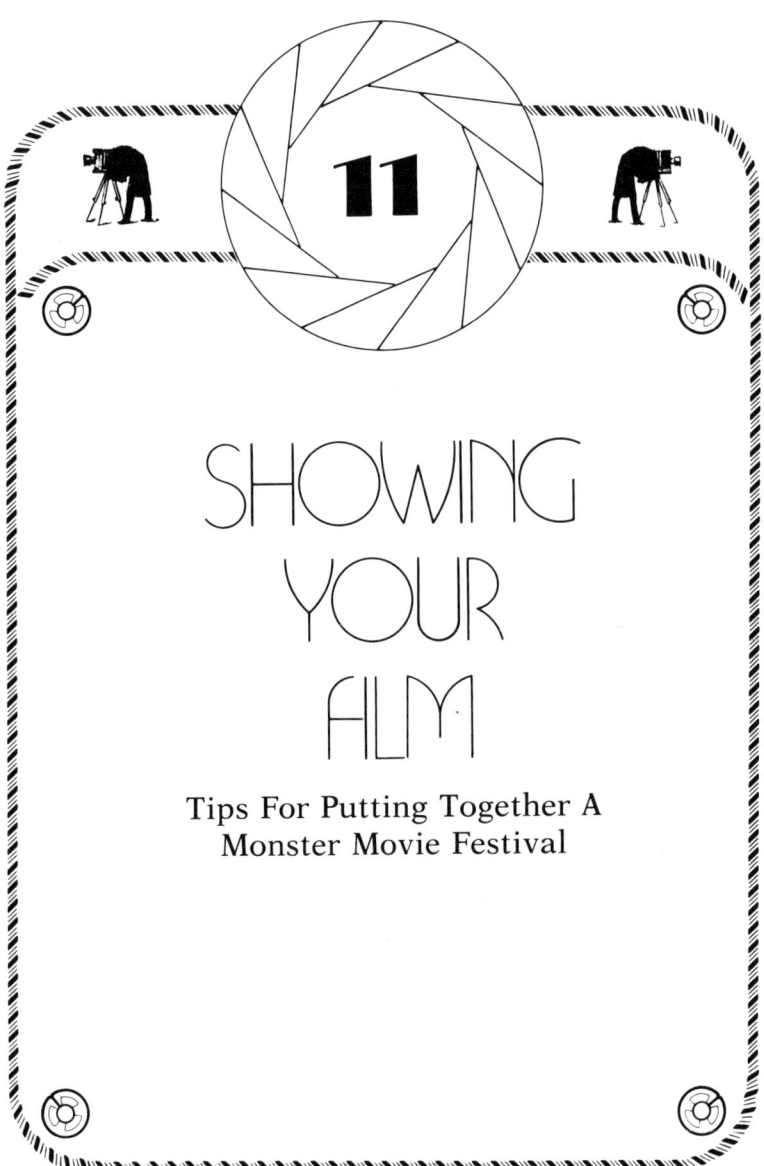

11

SHOWING YOUR FILM

Tips For Putting Together A
Monster Movie Festival

At last your movie is completed. You've worked long and hard to make it as good as possible and a good picture deserves a good audience. One way to attract a crowd to your film, and to make some money at the same time, is to put on a monster movie festival.

Here's All You Need To Do:

Find a place to show your film. A large, empty garage, a living room, or any room that can hold from 10–50 people, will do.

Gather together your equipment. This means you'll need a projector, a screen, a recorder or phonograph for your sound, a table to place the projector on, and a number of chairs and benches for your guests to sit on.

Pick a date and a time. Friday or Saturday night, early in the evening, will probably be best.

Prepare a poster or flyer advertising your festival. Be sure to include the date, time, name of the film, and place the film will be shown on the poster. If you have one, add a scary picture or drawing to the poster. Have photocopies of the poster made at a printer. Stick your advertisements up around your neighborhood. Perhaps some businesses in your area might post them in their windows. Mail others to friends and relatives. Send some to local newspapers and television stations with an accom-

panying letter—just a short note will do. Perhaps they'll give you a little free publicity. A sample poster might look something like the one above.

Charge admission to your festival. People will gladly pay to see your picture, especially if you charge something reasonable like a dollar or two. You deserve to make some money. You worked long and hard and spent some of the money, too. It is only fair that you get rewarded for your efforts.

And don't forget to serve refreshments. Popcorn is easy to make and so are drinks like lemonade and orange juice. In Hollywood, monster movies are sometimes known as popcorn pictures. That is because theaters sell extra popcorn every time they run these scary pictures. Theater owners say that the more scared and nervous people are, the more they seem to eat, perhaps to take their minds off their fear. So be prepared to make a little extra money on your bags of popcorn and drinks.

If you really want your festival to be first class, consider decorating your theater like a haunted house, Dracula's castle, or some other frightening location. Decorations need not be expensive. Things like bats cut out of construction paper and hung from the ceiling by thread, and pictures of monsters cut from monster magazines and tacked to the walls may be all you need to set a creepy atmosphere. At the entrance to your theater, put a sign that advertises your place as the ghoulish theater it is. Call it the Cobweb Cinema, Monster

Movie Palace, Dr. Frankenstein's Film Emporium, or think up your own name.

Put some eerie music or scary sounds such as screams and moans on a tape recorder and have it playing as your guests file in. If you are going to introduce your film, dress in a scary costume, perhaps one from the picture. Remember, the people who come have paid to be scared. Don't disappoint them.

When the film is over and the theater has been cleaned up, count your money. You should have made enough to cover the costs of making your movie. With luck you took in enough to pay for your next film as well.

Whatever you do, don't stop now. Your friends and fans are eagerly awaiting your next monster epic.

Keep making movies. You can only get better. Your first film may have just frightened the people in your neighborhood, but if you keep at it, you may someday find yourself making movies that will have people all over the world screaming in fear and panic. That's something to shoot for!